Inspirational Inner Wisdom

Unlock your inner wisdom
and be guided on your path.

Daily messages to inspire, uplift
and guide you forward on your journey.

MELISSA GIBBONS

BALBOA
PRESS
A DIVISION OF HAY HOUSE

Balboa Press books may be ordered through booksellers or by contacting:

Balboa Press
A Division of Hay House
1663 Liberty Drive
Bloomington, IN 47403
www.balboapress.com.au
1 (877) 407-4847

Printed in the United States of America.

ISBN: 978-1-4525-1216-7 (sc)
ISBN: 978-1-4525-1222-8 (e)

Balboa Press rev. date: 01/20/2014

This book, with love and light, is for all who dare to
seek and for all who are willing to go within, sit, be still
and use their awareness for their highest good.

This book is also for everyone who has a dream. Keep dreaming,
believe in yourself and know you can achieve your dreams!

For my children, Seth, Ryan and Kai, whom I tell every day:

Magic is real if you believe.

Contents

Foreword

Dear one, create awareness within yourself, let your spirit be free, dance to the beat of your drum, and go forth and be free. Use this beautiful treasure to help guide you on your way. Be strong, be courageous and use your awareness for your highest good.

Sit now, dear one. Bring your awareness to this present moment, be still, breathe and turn the book to the page you feel drawn. Read the guidance, trust that this message was given to you today with love and light and know there is treasure to be found within the words of this message. Let this message soak into your soul and feel where it resonates with you. Feel its vibration, feel its guidance and let it walk with you on your path.

Use this book daily, for the inspiration you will find within its pages will help you to unlock your own inner wisdom and who knows what treasure you may find there.

With love and light,
Melissa Gibbons

About Melissa

Melissa has a strong connection with the angels and has worked with them to channel and bring you powerful but gentle messages. These messages are from your angels to help you shift your perspective and go deep within yourself to heal, release, change your beliefs and live without limitations.

My Journey

How did I become involved in the work I do today?

I come from a very abusive background. My relationship with my mum was toxic and my dad was a biker who was consumed by that life. My parents split when I was 18 months old, my childhood was hell and at 14 I moved in with my dad.

At that point in time my dad had just had a major bike accident. He had nearly died, which was frightening, and his girlfriend was too controlling for me! So, at 16 I decided I was moving away from home to start my own journey into the world. I was naïve, depressed, lonely and scared, and where did I move to? Sydney! Of all places!

I moved into a refuge with drug addicts and prostitutes! I was neither of those things, but I could never be told what to do and hated authority. I had to work this world out on my own and navigate myself through whatever experiences life was bringing me.

I travelled to Queensland and New South Wales in the two years I was out of Melbourne and had lots of different experiences. But I wasn't happy. I was suffering severe depression and was diagnosed with borderline obsessive compulsive disorder. I used to get lost in TV shows and used them as my escape from reality in a very unhealthy way.

I finally needed rescuing at age 18 because I had run out of money. Dad came and rescued me and took me back to Melbourne. His girlfriend at the time introduced me to meditation and some things spiritual, which started me on my path of self-discovery.

I had always felt different and that I had a big mission to complete, though I didn't know what or how. I felt like the black sheep of my family and they reflected this back to me. Somewhere in all the chaos, though, I had my head screwed on and I knew I was destined for bigger and better things.

This didn't take away the pain, though, nor the hurt and anger I was harbouring towards my parents, my family and myself. I was a living, breathing, ticking time bomb of emotions that I didn't know how to deal with, and I really felt helpless. What I also didn't know was that I was about to discover a whole new world, a world that would educate me and give me positive tools to work with and apply in my life, and which would eventually lead me to become emotionally free!

My turning point

At 18 I was introduced to Reiki and my journey began. One thing led to another and I couldn't get enough; my world was opening up and it gave me an opportunity to take responsibility for my actions and my life. I had the opportunity to begin my healing journey, work through my issues and create my own philosophy and beliefs based on my own experiences.

I believe that if I have made it this far – and I have been in some dark, dark spaces mentally, physically and emotionally – anyone who is prepared to go deep within themselves and take responsibility for their own actions; anyone who is committed to themselves and is willing to shift their perspective and be open; and anyone receptive to change can create magic, healing and opportunities to live emotionally free. They can each become an amazing, empowered individual!

My life purpose

So, after some very deep healing work and pulling my life apart, I sit here as the person you see before you today. I have worked on a very deep level and completed many different healing modalities, but it is only in the last five years that I have known my purpose. That purpose involves helping women to heal and go on inner journeys within themselves to bring about massive, powerful and purposeful changes to live emotionally free and empowered lives.

I am real and what you see is what you get. I live and breathe my life purpose every day and I teach my children about the way I live and my beliefs. I have been blessed with three beautiful yet very individual children, two of whom have special needs, which has pushed me to grow immensely. Because of them I have been driven to go deeper in my work to see how I can help them; this is what led me to develop a range of consciousness sprays and go to places I never thought possible.

How I can help you

My business is based around my personal life experiences. I offer healings using a range of different modalities: Reiki, crystals and sound healings. I offer soul intuitive readings, where we go within to see what is holding you back on an emotional level and stopping you from moving forward. I also offer workshops and I am in the process of creating my own signature collection of healing tools.

I teach people how to remove their emotional blocks, deal with their emotions and become emotionally free to live an authentic life that is true to them. If I can do it, you can too. I believe in trusting your intuition, your own inner guidance and your truth.

I have fully surrendered my life over to the universe and the angels, and in doing so I just love my life. I am real! I am me! I can't hold my vibration high all the time, and neither will you be able to, but when you have awareness and the right tools, it's amazing how you can pull yourself up from anything.

I don't believe in pushing my opinions or truths onto others and I also say to people if you don't resonate with me as a healer or teacher, please find someone else. I wish only to attract people in line with my vibration, for these are the people I can genuinely help. I will not be offended if you don't resonate with me, my beliefs or my teachings as I know you are your own person and have your own truth and path to follow.

I will be honest with you always and everything I offer to you I am passionate about. I live and breathe my stuff daily; I walk my talk and I speak my truth. I am real and understand what it's like to go through real pain, abuse, hurt and heartache. I have been there in that place and to this day I continue to have my struggles, so I won't lie and tell you I can hold my vibration high all of the time because I simply can't. The difference is that when something comes up for me I face it, use my tools and work through it, which pushes me to constantly learn, grow and heal. Healing is like an onion: we are constantly peeling layers back and we are never not going to have something to work on. It's up to us to decide we will work on it, empower ourselves and not let our fears hold us back. We need to be constantly striving to move forward.

Thank you for letting me share my story with you.

Many blessings,
Melissa Gibbons

How to Use This Book

This book is a gift from my heart to yours. I have created this book to inspire and send positivity out into the world, for I believe every action creates a ripple effect and my hope with this book is to create a positive ripple effect of love.

My hope is for you to use this book every day just by opening it to one page – any page, specific or random – and reading the message and the power words there. The message will give you guidance about where your blocks are and give you positive thoughts to start your day. Trust that using this book will give you the perfect message every time and that it will be just what you need to hear in the perfect moment.

Use your awareness and intuition to decode the message for yourself and to identify what it means for you in your life. Trust the message even when you don't quite understand it. These messages are gentle reminders for your soul. This book asks you to trust and use your intuition, and to start to incorporate positive messages into your day.

Most importantly play and have fun, listen to your intuition, follow your heart and trust your gut. Live authentically and be honest with yourself. Keep in mind that we are all human and make mistakes, and that is perfect. Learn from your experiences; you don't have to be perfect and you are exactly where you are meant to be. Have trust, faith and hope, believe in magic, and nurture yourself.

Divine timing will take you on a journey. Practise patience, kindness and compassion; enjoy your journey; learn and grow from your experiences; and always honour yourself.

Enjoy this book, your gift with love from me to you. May it bring you peace, happiness and awareness.

Love and blessings,

Mel

Connection to Self

Core, coming back into self, being present, connecting with the knowledge that lies within

Connect, dear one. Come home to self and come back to the inner knowingness of your very being.

Come here, dear one. Sit with yourself, connect into your body, come home and come into your space. How do you feel connecting to the wisdom that lies within you? Ask yourself, dear one, are you connected to yourself? Have you been connected to yourself? Or are you disconnected from yourself?

Connection comes into our lives when we are gently being reminded to come back within and connect to ourselves. Connection is a word that links together all the pieces of our inner being that we have let go.

This message asks you to reconnect to yourself and embrace all the parts of you that need healing, releasing and accepting. It's ok, dear one. This gentle reminder asks you to reconnect with yourself. If you are not connected, what is stopping you or holding you back from connecting to your inner being and the divine wisdom that lies within you?

Connection to Self Power Words

With your hands on your heart say

I am connected to myself; I call all parts of myself back. I am connected to my inner wisdom and act accordingly.

Releasing

Release. Feel how you really feel. Raw, honest emotion pours from deep down inside.

Dear little one, it's time to release all that is stopping you moving forward. Call upon your inner strength and honour the feelings you have inside. These feelings are yours and you are allowed to feel them. Release, dear one; release the binds that hold you back.

Releasing has come into your life because it is time to release all emotions that no longer serve you or your purpose and it's time to release them in a way that makes your body feel good. If you want to get mad, get mad: yell, scream, let it out. It's ok, angel, to be messy. If you want to cry then cry, angel. Let the tears flow from you like the river that flows constantly. If you need to retreat, retreat. But know this, angel, those feelings you hold inside can no longer hide. It is time to acknowledge them and release them to the heavens, God and the angels for transmutation.

Release without fear. Release without judgment.

Releasing is a gift that helps you to move on and release stored up energy held within that holds you back from moving forward. It is safe for you to release. These emotions no longer serve you.

Releasing Power Words

Say this with your hands on your heart

I am willing to release all that no longer serves my highest good. I release doubt, I release fear and I release self-sabotaging thoughts. I replace them with loving thoughts and positive messages.

Womb Space

Come home, dear one. Come back within and centre deep into your womb space. You are now home.

Feel, dear one; feel into your body. How do you feel being present in this space? You can no longer run from yourself because you have been gone for far too long. It's time now, dear one, to come home and acknowledge self.

Coming home, dear one, can be the hardest thing we have to do. Sit and put your hand on your womb space, take a deep, long, continuous breath and breathe in and out. Acknowledge how you feel when you are home. Try to sit here as long as you can and feel into the space. How you feel in this space is a good indicator of where you are on your healing journey. Remember, in perfect time and space when you are ready you will heal. Right now you are creating awareness in yourself that will eventually lead to a shift in consciousness that is inevitable when you come home to self. Home is where you belong. Be gentle, dear one. With gentle persistence you will eventually feel safe and good about being home.

Womb Space Power Words

Place one hand on your heart and one hand on your womb space.
Stay there, feel into the feeling and come home, then say

*I am home, I am safe, I love myself completely
and it is safe for me to be home. When I am home
I am present and aware of my entire being, the
inner and outer, the thoughts and feelings. I now
know where I need to go within myself to heal
and release, for when I am home I am
connected to all of me.*

Lightning

Big, fast, unavoidable changes

Lightning has come to shake the very ground you walk on and burn right through to your very core.

Lightning is not gentle, dear one; it comes down with a bolt of force, striking with great power. Be prepared, for lightning brings great change with a driving, unstoppable force.

When lightning comes into your life, things move fast and often you really don't have a choice in the matter, for things can no longer stay as they are. Things will never be the same again.

Dear one, please do not resist these changes even if they scare you right down to your very core. Lightning has come to you because you have been hiding out and avoiding the inevitable. You know, dear one, as you have always known, you can no longer avoid this change, for the universe has made a decision to propel you forward for your highest good. Know this outcome is for the best and divinely inspired by the universe. Support yourself and nurture yourself through this change, for the decisions that lie before you are life-changing. Now it's time to go forth with blind faith and trust in the unknown, but remember your intuition and your gut are your most powerful resources. Listen to them and trust in them, and you shall find your way through the rumble to the peace and serenity you desire.

Lightning Power Words

Put your hands on your heart and say

I safely move through all changes with ease and grace. I am safe as I embark on this journey of change.

Power Pose

Find your power pose, step up and lovingly assert yourself now.

Dear one, you have kept yourself hidden for too long. You have a unique and special energy that the world needs at this time. It's time to step up, find your power pose and come out to the world!

Practise your power pose for two minutes a day. Feel it and breathe into this pose. Feel strong, assertive and confident and soon you will naturally become this: a confident, assertive person radiating beauty from within. This person emerges from the depths hidden down below. This person has always been there, they have never left, but they have just been hidden away and suppressed by circumstance, fear and judgment.

It is ok to be the bright, loving person you are and to be assertive as long as you come from your heart space.

Get in touch with your inner power today and practise your power pose. When you allow yourself to do this you will blossom like a flower coming into bloom, for when you practise and embrace your power pose, your life changes. Choose a power pose, angel, and strike your pose onto the world with love and grace.

Power Pose Power Words

Put your hands on your heart and say

I now stand tall. It is safe for me to be powerful.
I am powerful and confident. I now
step into my light.

Practise your power pose and step out into your light with
power and grace, knowing you are deserving in every way.

Dream Space

Immerse yourself in your dream space. When you go here, what do you dream?

Being in your dream space nurtures your soul, for being in this space lays the foundations for the life you want to create.

What you can dream for yourself, you can create!

Dream space comes to you to remind you that all dreams start with a thought, a thought that fills your heart with great joy, fills your soul with hope and thrusts you forward into passion.

Dream space fills your heart with joy, for when you are in your dream space you are thinking, feeling and creating the life you want to live, have, feel and touch. I ask you, dear one, why does this life have to be limited to your dream space? If you can dream it, you can create it!

Ask yourself, dear one, what is holding you back from bringing forth your dream space into reality?

What is it, dear one, what is it? Sit with this question, journal your thoughts down or talk with someone you trust who will help you to get to the bottom of what is holding you back.

What do you believe is holding you back from creating your dream space in the physical reality? For if you dream it, dear one, it's already there waiting for you to take steps towards your dream and create it in the physical world. Go forth into your dream space and create it. It's ok, dear one, go; go forth now!

Dream Space Power Words

Put your hands on your heart and say

I create my dreams with ease. My dreams are my passion and I easily create them. My dreams are my light, which guides me to my happiness. I am worthy of my dreams. My dreams create my inner light.

Inner Urgency

Listen to your soul, dear one. Are you at peace or are you restless? Do you feel you have an inner calling? Is there something that you have always known about but only now have an inner urgency to see manifest?

Dear one, this message has come into your life because you have a gift, a special and unique gift that you must share and bring forth into the world. Your inner light is spinning like an alarm and it is ringing and ringing; your soul yearns for you to fulfil your purpose. This calling will not stop, dear one, it will only intensify. Your current position in life, while it may be satisfying and safe, no longer brings you joy, for your inner urgency is calling you and gently nudging you to come forth, bring your unique gift and talent to the surface and share it with the world.

Yes, dear one, you may think to yourself, 'This path is not safe; it's not secure. Can I really make money doing what I love?' The answer is YES, dear one, you can and you need to bring forth your gift and share it with the world, for you are a powerful light worker and now is your time to come forth and take your place in the world. When you let go and step into your joy, sharing your gift and wisdom with the world, things will flow abundantly and you will never lack.

Have faith and trust in the unknown, for once the inner urgency has come forth you will need to find the courage to move forward in your calling. You know what that calling is, dear one; you have always known, for it has always been there, lying in your heart, calling you gently and now it's an inner urgency that you can no longer deny.

Nurture your dream, for everything is possible. Ease into your inner calling and things shall flow effortlessly and naturally, for you are a powerful light worker. Remember this, dear one. Let your gift glow and illuminate in the physical realm, supporting you and bringing you joy, abundance and growth on all levels.

Inner Urgency Power Words

With your hands on your heart say

I honour myself always, I acknowledge my inner urgency, I acknowledge my gifts and I choose to use them now.

Inner Wisdom

Dear one, dear one, you hardly know that which lies within you dormant and untouched, for what lies within you is magic untouched.

Dear one, please listen very carefully. Come close to me and listen as I whisper in your ear, for this you need to know, for this you need to hear.

You are so loved and supported, and you are never alone. All you ever need to know is hidden within you, lying dormant, still, stagnant and untouched. Just think for a moment, if you held all the answers what power would you hold? What knowledge would you possess? Would this lead to great riches or are you scared to look inside? The knowledge you seek is hidden inside of you, lying there for you to seek. Journey within, dear one, for you hold the key to unlocking the answers that you seek.

'Me?' you say looking through surprised eyes. 'But I am unclear, indecisive, inconsistent and clumsy at my best. How do I hold the key to the answers that I seek?'

I touch your shoulder, dear one, and ask you to come near. 'Have you heard a word that I have said?' I ask. 'What lies within you is the wisdom you seek. You hold the key to every question about yourself that you could ever want to know. You know the words that you want to speak, for this is your soul lying deeply in there before you. Do you dare to tap into the magic you seek? You think that all answers lie outside of you and come from everywhere else, when really all along the wisdom lay inside of you, waiting for you to seek it.'

This is your life; this is your soul. Tap into the wisdom, that inner wisdom you seek. It is inside of you; you and you alone have the answers you seek.

Inner Wisdom Power Words

Put your hands on your heart and say

I have infinite wisdom within me. I choose to learn from this wisdom and I use it now. I use the key to unlock the wisdom of my soul. This wisdom safely guides me on my journey. I trust my inner wisdom and I share it with others.

Exercise

Move, create, release

Dance, yoga, Thai Chi, walking

Exercise dear one, but engage only in exercise that brings joy, positivity, release and peace to your soul.

Tap into your intuition for, truth be told, you need to exercise your soul. Exercise helps discipline the mind and soul, and release pent up anger and other stored emotions that no longer serve you. Never do exercise out of obligation. Tune in to your intuition, tap into your body's wisdom and ask it for a message, for it will guide you to the exercise it seeks.

It's time to exercise, dear one, as movement brings about flow and flow ushers in positive new ideas and energy; releases stuck, stagnant energy; and brings in abundance and creativity in the form of ideas and inspiration.

Find some exercise you love today and move in the rhythm of creation, flow and peace. You will get new creative ideas and inspiration while filling yourself full of vital life force and pushing yourself to where you never dreamed you would go. Start gently and remember the flow.

Exercise Power Words

Put your hands on your heart and say

I use exercise to help clear old, stagnant energy and toxins from my body. Exercise brings my body, mind and spirit into harmony and connects them as one. I do exercise; I enjoy it and it nourishes my soul.

Breath

Mastering your breath is the first step in mastering your life.

Breath, dear one, is our vital life force; breath holds so much power within our bodies.

The way we breathe gives so much away about our wellbeing and peace of mind. We must learn to breathe correctly, for breath connects us to source.

Breath is all powerful and when we learn to master our breath we then awaken another force within us.

Try this exercise, dear one, for we must first learn to breathe correctly before we can master the power of breath.

To breathe correctly you must breathe in deeply through your nose and let your lungs fill with air. Feel your tummy draw up as you breathe in deeply. Your tummy will expand up and fill with air right down into your solar plexus, sacral and root chakras.

Then exhale, letting the air out, feeling your tummy sink into your spine as you exhale the stale air.

Practise this: inhale and let your belly rise; exhale and let your belly fall and sink into your spine, exhaling all the stagnant air out of your lungs.

Breath connects you to source. It calms and relaxes your body and helps you go into a meditative and relaxed state.

Breath is so very important. Practise this breathing exercise regularly and become the master of your breath today.

Breath Power Words

Put your hands on your heart and say

I breathe. I remember to breathe. I master my breath and then I master my life!

Hold Your Space

Compassion, love, acceptance, kindness, non-judgment, radiating love from the very core of your being, your heart space

Dear one, come into your heart space and feel the magnificent power that dwells within there. This is your heart space. Drop down into your heart space and see the world through eyes of love.

When heart space comes to you, you are being asked from this day forward to approach all situations from your heart space.

Dear one, when you speak and act with words of love from your heart space, you are coming from a place of truth and integrity. You will radiate love and you will deliver your message with authenticity. No matter what lies before you only love will exist and situations will work with you and not against you. Love is the purest form of expression. Today and for all of your tomorrows, approach situations and people with love, truth, honesty and integrity, coming from the loving space of your heart. For, when you let the bitterness, the anger, the fear, the resentment and the pain go, and you speak and see with love, you will realise that love is all that is and anything else is just an illusion.

Lead by example, dear one, and flow into your heart space. Become the flowing river that spreads love around the shores of the places you walk and touch. When you are in your heart space there is no room for casting judgment, fear or lack upon anybody because you see only through the eyes of compassion and love. You always approach interactions through the eyes and actions of love.

Dear one, you are being asked to hold your own space. Holding your own space transforms your whole vibrational essence. When you learn to hold your space you become a truly amazing being of wisdom, light and grace.

Holding your space, dear one, means becoming the wise sage you are. It means keeping secrets for the greater good and supporting yourself. When you own your space, you become your number one biggest supporter. Holding your space will help you to become an amazingly empowered human being and will open you up to the highest wisdom of the earth. It means holding on to secrets or knowledge that you alone should know. When you hold your space, dear one, you are building character and stamina, and you are creating inner strength, which is magic in its purest form.

When this message comes to you, it's asking you to hold your own space, recognise limitations, understand who you can and can't trust, and know you can always count on and trust yourself. This is holding your space.

You transition into the warrior and move forward knowing that when you hold your space you are steadfast in your position. You hold wisdom and your magic has risen to the surface in the purest form, dear one. It's coming and soon you will realise what holding your space means to you. You will then hold your space with poise and grace, like the majestic lion poised for success.

Keeping knowledge, secrets, faith and belief inside yourself while living your life for your highest good is holding your own space. Holding your own space means you have come full circle or are about to come full circle and live with conviction, trusting your gut and living in your power. You, dear one, are so powerful now because you know what it means to be holding your own space.

Strong wise one, we send you love from the divine directly into your heart.

Hold Your Space Power Words

Put your hands on your heart and say

*I hold my space, I honour my wisdom and
I honour everybody else's wisdom. I hold space
for myself and others really well.*

Creator

Awareness, becoming awake so we can implement and facilitate change in our lives and be the creators of our lives

This message has come to you today to tell you that you are a powerful creator; every day you are creating on the canvas called life.

You, dear one, are the powerful creator of your life, a living, breathing example of art. What are you creating, dearest one? Think about the words that you speak: your self-talk, how you speak about others and your views on life itself. With the awareness of yourself being the creator, are you really creating all that you seek, all that you desire and all that nourishes your soul? Are you the creator of joy, love, peace and happiness? Are you creating the canvas of the life that you seek?

If you become present and aware, dear one, of the words you speak, your thoughts and your actions, then you can change them to support you and help create the very life you seek. For, as the creator, you hold great power. Everything you do and say is creating the canvas of your life. The universe is reflecting back to you how you think and see the world; this is powerful, dear one. Think about your life. Think about what you attract into your life. Are these situations, people and things you want, or are they reflections of what you speak and how you think and act? Dear one, when you realise you are the creator and you create the experiences you seek, you can begin to change the very canvas your life plays out on. You hold the power; do with it as you wish. But, dear one, you hold the power. Are you creating the canvas that you seek?

This message asks you to become fully aware of your actions, words, fears, thoughts, self-talk, how you speak of others and how you treat yourself and others. These are all reflections of your current circumstance. At any given moment you hold the power to change this canvas. Accepting responsibility for your actions, thoughts and beliefs will help you to see through the eyes of awareness.

The most powerful moment in your life is when you realise you hold the power within yourself to create the change and life you seek. It is never too late to start; we must just first be willing to move forward without looking back.

You are a powerful creator from this day forth. Make a commitment to create your life with positive intent.

Creator Power Words

Place your hands on your heart and say

I am a powerful creator. I create deliberately and with intent. I am creating the life I desire. I create effortlessly and easily every day.

You Have Permission

Dear one, this is your life and you are living it. Up until now you have made decisions and choices that have led to this very spot, yet you sit here before me missing something. Are you waiting for permission?

As you sit here wanting something, feeling like something is missing from your life, ask yourself who told you that you couldn't do it? Who told you that you were not good enough or deserving enough? Who is holding you back and stopping you from moving forward in your life?

Dearest one, you have permission. It is safe for you to move forward on your journey and bring into your life that which you wish to create. Oh, dear one, stop holding yourself back based on idle words and idle threats. Those words were said long ago yet they are implanted in your mind like seeds planted into the earth and you nourish them and give them water to grow, though they are but weeds of your mind that you must let go.

You now have permission, dear one, from this time and space to move forward and create your dreams. Listen to nobody for their utterances are just words, simply a reflection of the speaker's own life and the fears they hold inside, passed on to you like a dis-ease, creating fear in your very being and acting like a force that has held you back.

It is time to cut the cords to these reflections, this fear, this hurt and this grief that has held you back from moving forward for far too long. You have permission now, though you have never needed permission, dear one. Knowing you have always had permission, you can now choose to reach out and take it. Give yourself permission to move forward without fear, without shame and without guilt, for you are worthy and deserving of having everything you want and more.

You have permission. If this message has come to you today, somewhere in life someone has put you down, hurt you, projected their own fear onto you and cut you down from the knees. This was somebody else's fear, hurt, guilt, shame, resentment or bitterness pushed onto you. Know from this moment forward, dear one, you have complete permission to move on and create the life of your dreams. You are worthy and deserving of this.

Sit with one hand on your heart and the other on your womb space. Breathe into this and feel it – really feel it. Now ask yourself, who told you that you couldn't? Who told you that you were not good enough or deserving enough? Or perhaps somebody said something different that was still just as hurtful. Breathe into this and the first person who comes to mind will be the person you need to cut cords from, release, forgive and heal.

You Have Permission Power Words

Put your hands on your heart and say

I give myself permission to be happy now. I give myself permission to receive now. I give myself permission to be abundant now. I give myself permission to receive love now. I open my arms and allow myself permission to receive.

Decision

It's time to make a decision, dear one, but this is not just any decision, this is the decision of your life!

Decision in Latin means to kill off other options. This decision you have before you is a life-changing one, one that must be made when your heart and gut are in sync and you have great clarity within your mind's eye.

Indecision, dear one, leads you to be stuck, stagnant and unable to move forward. This creates lack, fear, resentment, bitterness and dis-ease within the body. It's time, dear one, to make your decision. Feel into your heart space and learn to trust your gut.

This message has come to you because you need to make a decision that is based on three things:

1) Trust
Trust your gut and know that this is just right. You don't need to know all the facts, hows and whys, you just need to make a decision and the rest will follow. Trust this.

2) Clarity
You need to be clear about what you want and go for it. When you become clear without hesitation the universe will respond by making this happen, things will flow and fall into place very easily.

3) Heart
This decision has to bring you great joy. It's what you want, it's what you've always wanted and this decision fills your heart up with joy. It is heart-based and loved-based, not based on fear.

Trust, dear one. Let go of the fear and lack that comes with indecision. Make this decision so it's your only option; once this decision is made there is no other option. This is a power process in making decisions. Use this process to help you make decisions in your life today and watch how when you use this process magic happens.

Dear one, this process calls for trust, clear faith and complete heart-based belief in what you are doing. This is part of the process; without these three things the decision process won't work. You must be committed and dedicated to your decision. Remember trust, clarity and heart as well as complete faith and belief are essential to making a decision.

This process is powerful and will help you move mountains in your life. You need to be your number one biggest supporter and only share your decisions with supportive people or keep them to yourself. Fear, insecurity and lack of trust, faith and belief will hold you back. There comes a time in life when we must step up, step away from fear, doubt and disbelief, and each trust our own gut and follow our own heart.

Fear is ego. Don't let ego talk you out of achieving your dreams. You so deserve this, so empower yourself now to make decisions with clarity and ease.

Decision Power Words

Put your hands on your heart and say

I make decisions with ease and with clarity.

Trust Your Gut

Dear one, you are intuitive, you are connected to source and you are guided by source and all that is. We now ask you to trust your gut.

Your gut is an accurate barometer of truth. You get gut feelings all the time but how often do you act on them?

We, dear one, want you to trust in your gut and trust in yourself. Not only are you accurate in what you feel right in the very centre of your solar plexus but by not trusting it and being in resistance, you are shutting this energy centre down. It is time to come back to centre and trust your gut, for when you do magic happens and things start flowing.

This message comes to you because you are being urged to trust your gut. It is so accurate and spot on; how many times have you kicked yourself in the past for not following through on something your gut was telling you?

It's time to reopen this energy centre – this powerhouse – and become empowered by trusting your gut, your accurate barometer of truth. Trust your gut today for it's the truth and will always connect you to your highest good. The angels ask you, dear one, are you trusting in your gut today?

Think about this question, dear one, and come back to centre in yourself. Come home and ask yourself, are you trusting your gut? It's time to trust your gut from now on, dear one. Make a commitment to trusting your gut today.

Trust Your Gut Power Words

Put your hands on your heart and say

I trust my intuition and follow my intuition always. My gut is my truth and my heart will reflect this truth always. I listen to and trust them and follow them always.

Body Wisdom

Dear one, it's time to tune in to your body and ask it for a message. Your body has all the answers you seek. In fact, every minute of every day, your body is communicating with you – giving indications, feelings and messages – and asking you to tune in to what it is telling you. Your body is your best friend and it is so wise; listen to your body today!

Sit quietly and breathe deeply into the core of your very being. Notice where you are holding tension, where you are sore, any health problems you may have and any tightness in any one area of the body. All these problems started with emotions held within the body that you haven't been able to release, resulting in dis-ease of the body.

Don't beat yourself up over this; instead listen, really start to listen to your body. Consider how you are feeling and relate this back to your aches, pains and dis-eases of the body. When you do this you will create a map inside of you that can now tell you where you are on your healing journey and where you can begin to release and heal your emotions, and so turn dis-ease into ease and bring wellness back into your body.

When we speak of wellness, we speak of the whole body encompassing body, mind and soul – physical, emotional and spiritual. We want you to be in touch with your total wellbeing and know you can begin to heal from the inside out by using your emotions and symptoms as starting points. By all means go to your physician and don't stop taking medications but use this message to connect into your body and begin to heal your emotions, mind, body and spirit. This will mean taking guided action. Start slow, be gentle and go at your own pace. There is no rush here; all we ask is that you gently open up your mind to your body's wisdom, expand your awareness and take responsibility for your health and what you can do to help yourself.

Seek support from natural medicines, your local doctor and the community, embracing all that is out there and trusting your gut. There is no good, bad or wrong way to do this. You can't be wrong when you are trusting the messages your body is giving you and acting on them.

Go gently and get into a flow. This could mean you simply start by receiving a Reiki treatment, having a massage, taking a bath or reading a book. By doing this you bring more awareness to your body. You might also change your diet but start slow, do research before you make major changes, and become educated. Trust yourself and your body because it knows what to do.

We have a set of major energy centres in the body called chakras:

Crown. This is located at the top of the head and connects us to source. Its resonating colour is purple.

Third eye. Set in the middle of the forehead, this is our intuition. Its resonating colour is indigo.

Throat. This is at the centre of the throat and is about expression. Its resonating colour is blue.

Heart. This chakra is located where the heart is. Its resonating colour is green.

Solar plexus. This is in the middle of the tummy. Its resonating colour is yellow.

Sacral. This is set about 7.5 centimetres (3 inches) below the navel. Its resonating colour is orange.

Base chakra. This chakra is located just below the sacral chakra. Its resonating colour is red.

These energy centres need to be open to be working. If they are closed off or blocked they may affect your energy and health.

Become in tune with your body wisdom and decode its messages today.

Body Wisdom Power Words

Put your hands on your heart and say

I listen to my body, I understand its message and my body guides me to what I need now.

Relationship with Self

Dear one, this message comes to you to gently remind you that you must love and accept yourself, you must meet your needs, you must support yourself, you must encourage yourself, you must nourish yourself and you must treat yourself with respect and dignity.

Do you have a relationship with yourself? Are you meeting your needs and making yourself happy? Are you giving yourself love and support?

Ask yourself these questions, dear one, and be honest with your answers. It's time to get real and get grounded into reality.

In order for anybody to give you love, ask yourself, am I loving myself?
In order for anybody to make you happy, ask yourself, am I making myself happy?
In order for others to support you, ask yourself, am I supporting myself?
In order for others to help you, ask yourself, am I helping myself?
In order for others to respect you, ask yourself, am I respecting myself?

If you are not doing these things for yourself, how can anyone else do them for you? Wow, dear one. Powerful but true. No one else can meet your needs before you meet them yourself.

You must first develop a healthy relationship with yourself, meet your needs, and love and respect yourself before anybody else on this earth can do this for you.

This is the ultimate truth: until you develop a relationship with yourself that encompasses love, respect, help and support, a relationship where you really treat yourself how you want to be treated by others, how can you expect anybody on this earth to do this for you?

Angel, it's time you went about meeting your needs as a person, loving yourself, helping yourself, respecting yourself as a person, supporting yourself and doing all the things for yourself that you would like somebody to do for you.

When you meet all your needs, others will follow and treat you how you treat yourself. Then, dear angel, once love flows from inside of you and radiates out of you, you will attract great love, great support, great help and great respect from others. People will mirror back to you all that you are doing for yourself.

So, dear one, please develop a healthy, loving relationship with yourself first before attempting this with anyone else. When you do, love will be magnified in your life tenfold plus more and people will treat you how you wish to be treated because you are treating yourself this way.

When you have a healthy, loving and respectful relationship with yourself others will naturally treat you this way because you are setting boundaries around how you want to be treated that others will follow.

Relationship with Self Power Words

Put your hands on your heart and say

I love and respect myself. I treat myself lovingly and kindly with respect. I nurture my mind, body and spirit.

Support

Support is all around you, dear one. We are here supporting you and looking out for you. We want to help you, we want to see you succeed and we love you, dear one; we always have and always will. Nothing you could ever do or say will make us turn our love away; we're here for you every step of the way. We just need your permission to help you in your life. Give us permission. It's ok to ask us for help. We are not restricted by space and time; you are not taking us away from anybody else who needs us more because nobody needs us more than you do, angel. Talk with us, give us your worries, give us your cares, let us in to guide you and hold your hand, and feel our loving embrace around you and our warmth in your heart. These are all signs we are here.

The angels, Ascended Masters, goddesses, gods, fairies, spirits, nature sprites and guardian angels all dance around you, dear one. Give them your worries, cares, hopes and dreams and ask them to help.

This message has come to you today because many magical beings surround you, support you and love you but they need your permission to help you in your life. Call upon them today to help guide you in your life. There is nothing to fear, dear one, for the angels are near. These beautiful beings can help you in all areas of your life.

Invoke them into your life today; they are already here, they just need your permission. Remember, they have always been here, dear one. The thought that you are alone is only an illusion.

Magical beings dance around you bringing you signs every day that you are supported, loved and not alone. Open up and become aware of these signs, dear one. These signs might be feathers, dreams, songs on the radio or surprise opportunities that pop up. Someone may say something that you need to hear, you may be somewhere at the perfect time and place, or you may see sequences of numbers that repeat themselves. These are all signs that your angels are around you.

Open your consciousness to these signs and become aware of them, for the signs are confirmation that magical beings dance around you and are talking to you, guiding you and supporting you. Magic happens when you become aware of these signs. Heed them, let them embrace your entire being and fill you with love and warmth because, dear one, this is how we communicate with you.

Support Power Words

Put your hands on your heart and say

I am supported. I support myself in every way.
I accept support from others easily and
my needs are met.

Expression

Expression is the art of doing, talking, communicating, dancing, cooking, making music, writing, drawing or any activity that encourages you to express yourself. Talk, dance and be free, dear one, for your soul is longing for expression.

Express yourself through emotion, thought, belief, opinion and using your voice. Your soul is longing for you to express yourself now.

This message has come to you because it's time to find your voice, a safe space and an activity in which you can express and just be yourself. For too long you have kept yourself hidden inside and your beautiful soul is wanting to come out and be heard.

You have a gift of expression; all of humanity is waiting for you to express. When you express you bring joy, love, happiness, words of encouragement and words of hope that others need to hear, for it touches their souls and they find it healing. When you express yourself you are releasing their expression, which can be one of the most healing things you do. Your soul longs to release their expression.

Let the tears out, let the hurt out and let the emotions out. Give yourself permission to express, to be the person you want to be by using your expression. Expression is so important in this life; it's time for you to express. It's time for you to find your voice and speak up. For too long you have kept your voice hidden.

Through expression, dear one, you will find the piece that is lost, you will fill your heart with joy and you will create love, peace and happiness in the world for yourself and for all. With expression you can be all that you can be.

Find what you need to express today: release, healing, love, joy, abundance, peace, fulfilment, power or maybe something else.

It's your time to be heard. It's time to express your life.

Expression Power Words

Put your hands on your heart and say

I express myself with love. I am heard and I communicate my message easily and effectively.

Vision

You see visions through your mind's eye; you see visions in your sleep; you hold visions in your heart; for vision is what you seek.

Dear one, you are very connected to spirit, source and all that is, and you experience visions in all that you do and seek.

These visions, or downloads, are direct from source. How do you know they are pure in intent? It is because they come from love, peace and abundance, and fill your heart with joy. If your visions are fearful and filled with lack, loss and despair, then they are just ego and not from source; that is how you tell the difference.

You are being asked to trust and follow through on the visions you see that fill your heart with joy.

Ideas, inspiration and messages are being sent to you from the magical beings that dance around you and connect with you. They are sending you visions to behold. This message relates directly to your third eye, which sees through the eyes of spirit.

This is confirmation that you are very much in tune with the divine and connected to the magical beings of source. They constantly send you downloads in the form of visions and messages and they gently guide your hand and your heart.

You are a powerful light worker, dear one. You need you to bring these visions forth into the tangible universe. Bring forth your gift into the world: share, open people's hearts and minds, and bring awareness to the infinite impossibilities that exist.

Part of your mission is to help people believe, trust in and love all that is in themselves. Spirit is working through you. You are being asked to follow through and shine your light and gift onto the world. You are a clear vessel and spirit works through you.

Spirit is supporting you and gently nudging you to come out into the world. Spirit has chosen to work through you as a source connected to the divine. It is time to step up and do your work as a light worker. Congratulate yourself, dear one, for being a clear vessel that spirit and source can work through to get their message out into the world. You are the most perfect person to deliver this message and do spirit's work. Take guided action today.

Spirit thanks you and supports you while you are doing this work.

Namaste.

Vision Power Words

Put your hands on your heart and say

I easily see through my mind's eye. I trust in the images, the messages and the guidance I receive. I easily hear messages from source.

Cutting Cords

Your energy is precious, dear one. You are a magic energy magnet giving out and receiving energy each day. Spirit asks you to stop and think about this and asks ever so gently, are you protecting yourself, shielding yourself and cutting your cords, dear one?

At this moment, dear one, you are an energy power source giving out and receiving energy. You are a sensitive being, dear one, which means that people need and source your energy. Your energy is pure, positive and beautiful; you help others to feel good without even knowing it and others plug in and take from your energy source unknowingly. This happens on a subconscious level, but now it's time to become aware of your energy source, your powerhouse. You need to keep it clear and shining brightly like the midnight stars that light up the sky, and because you are sensitive, dear one, you need to honour your light and power source. You need to clear, protect, cleanse, cut cords and get rid of any things that, energetically, are not yours.

So, beautiful being, what are the signs and feelings that your energy source has been tapped into or invaded? Understand that you allowed this by lack of awareness of procedures to stop it, but know that that's ok. How can you know if you have not been made aware?

Every time we speak with somebody we create a cord from them to us. This also happens with situations, emotions and places we might go. These cords feed into each other; they are thick tubes with energy running through them that attach from you to a source, which might be a person, place or situation. Unless these cords are cut daily they constantly feed energy back and forth, whether positive or negative. We need to be aware of these cords so we can cut them and clear ourselves regularly to keep our energy clear and high.

When you have cords attached to you and don't cut your cords, dear one, you may have feelings of tiredness, exhaustion, aggravation or anger, or experience instant headaches that weren't there a moment ago. You might walk away from somebody or some situation feeling drained or just have an uneasy feeling. You can feel like there is a knot in your in your tummy or that you just don't feel right, or you may have tightness or aches in your body. Everybody is different, dear one, and will have different symptoms. Become aware of your symptoms, tune in to your body and make a mental note of how you feel when you have cords attached to your energy centre.

To help clear these cords you can work daily with Archangel Michael. Archangel Michael is a magnificent angel who has a sword to cut all your cords with. He also has an etheric vacuum, which he can place in your crown chakra to clean any toxicity from your system. You can also attach this vacuum to your solar plexus to infuse it with colour to re-energise your energy centres. Archangel Michael is the protector, he is good with electrical things, he is just beautiful and his colour is cobalt blue. All you have to do is ask him to come and help you cut your cords and send them up to the Violet Light for transmutation.

A message from Archangel Michael:

Hello, dear one. I am here with my sword. I am here to share with you my knowledge and my sword. Call on me, dear one, day and night to help you clear and purify your energy field so you may keep it bright and energised.

I find these things help and work for me. Archangel Michael is the most divine being and I work closely with him every day. Here are some techniques I use to help keep my vessel clear and shining bright that you might like to try:

Every morning when you wake up, just spend one or two minutes before getting out of bed setting up your energy shield for the day. You can imagine yourself in a beautiful white dress or suit. In front of you is a magnificent bubble. Step into that bubble. On the outside of the bubble is a mirror that lets all the positive energy come through and penetrate the energy bubble around you while reflecting all the negative energy directly back to the sender or source. Now imagine your bubble filling up with the most magnificent colours – any colours your heart desires; ones that make you feel good. Once that is done, put colours on the outside of your bubble. Start with visualising a cobalt blue light radiating out from the bubble and all around it. Next visualise silver around the outside of the bubble, followed by pink, by green and then by white light. Your energy is now protected for you to go out into the world.

At night before you go to sleep, call upon Archangel Michael to cut all your cords for that day, keeping in mind when we meet and chat with people we create cords that attach our energy field to theirs. Unless you cut these cords they keep filtering through energy, positive or negative.

Ask Archangel Michael to cut all cords from your day and to place his etheric vacuum onto your crown chakra to get rid of all toxic energy and pollutants from your day. He could also place his vacuum over your solar plexus to flow colour through to any parts of the body you feel may need rejuvenating. As the cords are being cut, see the cords being flicked into the Violet Fire for transmutation.

You can also call upon Archangel Raphael to come shine some green light where the cords have been cut. As some cords may feel like tree roots being pulled out, you may need Archangel Raphael's green light to soothe you where a cord has been cut.

Another tip Archangel Michael has asked me to pass on is if at any time, day or night, you are out somewhere and you instantly feel yuck after visiting a place, or talking to somebody or a group of people, this is an indication that you have taken on something from others. This is something that they needed to offload and isn't yours, but because you're a sensitive being you tend to take on other people's stuff and carry it within you.

In this situation all you need to do is say Archangel Michael, please take away anything that is not mine and send it up to the Violet Fire for transmutation. Instantly you will feel better.

These are the ritualistic practices I follow every day and they work for me. Find something that works for you and practise it daily.

Cutting Cords Power Words

Put your hands on your heart and say

*I easily see the patterns I need to let go of.
I release these patterns with ease as I move
forward on my journey, trusting that I
am on the right path.*

Power Words

Power words, dear one, are those words of love and encouragement that nourish your soul and mind and give you the strength, courage and motivation you need to go about your day.

Dear one, we ask you to use your power words every day. Use power words in self-talk and the way you talk about your situation and circumstance.

Power words are so all important. Think, dear one, what do you need to get through your day? How can you use your power words to stay focused and achieve your goals? You must continue to Round-Tree your power words in your head (that is my method for saying them over and over again to yourself) and believe every word you say.

Power words help bring us back to centre and make us feel safe in a world that can have us doubting the very ground we walk on. What are your power words? Use them today and every day.

There are many power words that you may choose to use. Be creative, dear one, and think of your own. If you think of them yourself they will have more meaning for you.

Here are some power words you might like to start with:

I am flexible
I am strong
I am safe and angels help to guide me
I am supported
I am loved
I can do this

Tune in to your gut, dear one. Each circumstance will be as different and individual as the next. Make your power words strong, short and to the point to help you get through those circumstances and situations you are struggling with every day.

Power Words

Sit, dear one, think about a situation in your life and then
make up your very own power words for the situation.
You can write them in the space below if you wish.

_____

_____

_____

_____

_____

_____

_____

_____

Clarity

Dear one, it's time to get clear: clear on your purpose and clear on the decisions you need to make. You need to move forward in your life with pure, clear intentions.

Dear one, it's time to get some clarity on a situation in your life. This message has come to you because the angels want you to be crystal clear from now on and clear the clutter in your mind, clear out ego and clear out fear. They are only distractions stopping you from getting clear and certain about the decisions you need to make in your life.

It's time to get clear in your head about how you want to proceed. Stay centred in your gut, do what feels right and get clear with no more doubt, no more fear and no more confusion. You know deep down in your gut what you want and how you want to proceed; it is time for action. Trust and use clarity to guide you through to the other side.

See through the eyes of clarity, dear one, for when you do this you will be clear and able to move forward with ease, grace and pure intent coming from your heart space. Know with conviction that you have come from a place of clarity.

Clarity Power Words

Put your hands on your heart and say

I have clarity in my mind, clarity in my heart and clarity in my soul. I act when I am clear on my intentions.

Create Your Space

Do you have a space? An altar? A special place just for you?

Dear one, it's time to create a space that is your space, a space where you can go to have sanctuary away from the daily grind of life. Fill your space with things you love and things you enjoy. Make this space a visually pleasing, safe place where you can meditate, write, ground your energy and rejuvenate. We all need a space, dear one. Have you created your divine, magical space where you can work your magic?

This message is also asking you to de-clutter your physical surroundings and get rid of the clutter in your mind as well as any physical junk you no longer need in your life. De-cluttering opens the way to usher in new positive energy and opportunities for you to create your magic. Nurture yourself in the de-cluttered space, dear one. This space is yours and yours alone. Use your space daily or go somewhere now that fills your heart with joy. Having a special, sacred space fills our entire beings with love and gratitude, and nourishes our souls.

Create Your Space Power Words

Put your hands on your heart and say

I create a space, a place for me to be. My space is beautiful, quiet and peaceful. I relax and just be in my space.

Use the Tools

This message asks you to draw upon your toolbox, bring your tools into the physical world and remember how powerful tools really are.

What tools resonate with you? Do you connect with crystals, books, angel cards, flower essences, meditation, listening to music, energy healing, journaling or something else?

Dear one, you are being asked to find and use tools that you are attracted to and can help you on your journey. Tools are there to support us and remind us that we can do this, that we are each here to walk our own journey, but that we are not alone and it is okay to find tools to support our wellbeing.

Invest in yourself today; tools are worth it because they can sometimes be our greatest asset, the driving force that keeps us moving forward. Ask yourself, dear one, what tools do you need in your life today? Invest in them for they will support you a thousandfold on your journey. They will give you access to strength and power on your darkest days and sometimes they will be the very thing that pulls you through.

Invest in some tools today to help you on your journey, but remember that investment doesn't just have to be money. Get creative: you can even make your own tools! If you invest time into them they will be magical because they were made by you and hold your essence and energy.

Hello Angel,

I would just like to add that tools are magical; they pick me up on my gloomy days and bring me back to centre. I have a whole roomful of tools and I play and create with each and every one of them. Don't deny yourself tools, dear one. They bring and create magic in your life. You have permission from me to invest in your toolkit today. I am eternally grateful for my large bag of tools; remember, they don't have to cost the earth.

Love and blessings,
Mel

Use the Tools Power Words

Put your hands on your heart and say

I have magic within me and all around me. I use this magic to facilitate my healing journey.

Intuition

You have a strong, grounded connection to the divine. You are an intuitive being of light.

Angel, you are so divinely connected, so divinely loved and so supported. Your intuition is strong, you just need to tune in and hone in to it like it's a signal beaming down from the heavens and guiding you home. Your strong, divine, powerful connection helps you to stay in touch with your intuition.

Your intuition is always there, angel; it will never abandon you. You just need to learn to tap into it and surrender to its rhythm and beat. Listen to and trust your intuition with conviction for you, dear one, are ever so connected to source. Let your intuition guide you like a shining light. Trust and follow your intuition today.

This message comes to you because you are divinely intuitive. Trust in, surrender to and follow your intuition from now on; it will not serve you wrong but it will guide you home. Your intuition is the most powerful resource you have. Learn to harness its power and use it in your life today.

Intuition Power Words

Put your hands on your heart and say

I have a strong, grounded intuition. I listen to and I am guided by my intuition. I trust it and follow it always.

Shift Your Perspective

It's time to shift your perspective and change your life.

Dear one, the angels are calling on you to shift and change your perspective. Look for the blessing in the situation and turn it into a positive. No matter what you are doing, when you learn and apply this technique to shift your perspective, magic happens.

Shift your perspective and transform your life. Magic really does happen when we shift from a negative to a positive perspective. Make this a rule for yourself: if you find yourself looking at a situation with a negative perspective, shift your conscious perspective to the positive. There is always a blessing to behold when we shift our perspective away from the negative. The angels urge you to shift from a negative to a positive perspective today.

Angel, I apply this rule to my life every day. I have a dog and I need to pick up dog doo on a regular basis. This is certainly not my favourite job; to be honest, I really dislike it and would rather someone else do it. But it's my job and I need to get it done, so I shift my perspective. I take off my shoes and say to myself, this is my time to ground and connect with nature, and I focus my energy on getting grounded and being in nature. I do this by really enjoying the barefoot sensation of being connected to Mother Earth through the grass. This makes me forget about picking up dog doo so that, even though it's not my focus, the job gets done and I get to enjoy nature and get grounded.

I now like picking up the dog doo. Why? Because I've shifted my perspective and made my focus about something else. It's now a magical time plus I get my job done. I have taken my perspective of picking up dog doo and shifted it so that instead of a yuck chore it's now my 5 to 10 minutes I spend outside getting grounded and enjoying nature each day. See how amazing the power of shifting your perspective really is?

I urge you, dear one, to shift your perspective on situations in your life today. Once you do this, magic happens. Try shifting all your perspectives on all situations that are negative and try making them positive today. Really practise this in your daily life and it will become second nature to you to be able to shift your perspective on any situation that happens in your life.

Shift Your Perspective Power Words

Put your hands on your heart and say

My mind and heart are open to new possibilities.
I let go of all judgments now.

Discipline the Mind

Shh, dear one, quieten down your mind. It's time to get strong, be strong, act strong and discipline your mind.

Dear one, discipline of the mind is fundamental to your wellbeing. It is now, dear one, that you are being urged to become familiar with this practice of disciplining the mind.

When we discipline our minds we become strong, we become focused and we become clear. When your mind is disciplined your energy is centred and grounded into the physical realm, you are in your body, you are strong and you are connected to all that is divine. Discipline your mind today and you will achieve all you desire plus more.

Angel, disciplining your mind will take practise, commitment, courage, trust and faith. You must practise every day the art of disciplining your mind. Your mind is an almighty powerhouse that you need to get on board to believe that you are strong, grounded and centred.

Once you discipline your mind you really can achieve anything because your mind will be sound, focused, accountable and present. It will become aware and start to respond to your will. Stop, angel, this is important: get into the daily habit of getting your mind focused, positive and strong. Discipline your mind and you will move mountains and achieve anything your heart truly desires.

Hello Angel,

I practise believing in myself and my ability to create a disciplined mind every day, and if you do too it will soon become second nature for you as well. I do this through the art of Bikram Yoga and I urge you to find an activity that helps you to discipline your mind. If my mind is not centred and strong within, I cannot complete my 90 minute open eyed meditation that is required in Bikram Yoga.

Yoga challenges me to be present in my body and focus my mind on what I am doing. I urge you, angel, to find an activity that will help you strengthen and discipline your mind; all this will help you in your everyday practice and you will get results.

Love,
Mel

Discipline the Mind Power Words

Put your hands on your heart and say

I master my mind and my thoughts. I learn to discipline my mind and become free of all fears and limitations.

Commitment

It's time to make a commitment to yourself. You are worth it.

Dear one, make a commitment to yourself today. Your lack of commitment to yourself up until now has blocked your progress; you need to decide to commit to yourself and your dreams today. No one else can commit to them for you. No one can serve you up commitment on a platter and make things happen for you. You and only you are responsible for implementing the change you want to see in your life. Take the angels' pledge of commitment today.

I, _____, today decide I give myself permission to be committed to myself and to do what I need to do to make my dreams come true. I commit to take steps to heal, grow, learn and expand my consciousness. I am committed to healing my life and all that is.

Today I declare that I am going to make a commitment to myself. I will follow this practice daily and ground myself in the physical universe. I commit to making the change that is necessary in my life, the change that I need right now. I am fully and wholeheartedly committed to myself today in the present moment.

Angel, now that you have taken the pledge, stick to it, embrace it, love it and do it. You are worthy and deserving of bringing about the changes in your life that your heart desires, and only you can bring them forth into the physical realm. Embrace your commitment today.

Commitment Power Words

Put your hands on your heart and say

I make a commitment to myself. I am worth it and I believe in myself and my dreams. I make a commitment to myself now.

Take a few moments to write out your commitment to yourself. You can use the space below if you like.

Angelic Communication

We angels are all around you, loving you, supporting you and guiding you. We ask you to notice our signs and acknowledge us today, for we are trying to communicate with you.

Dear one, every day your angels and guides are communicating with you. Do you know and recognise the signs? Are your eyes open? Are you listening for the whispers in your ear? Are you feeling the angels dancing around you? Open your heart to the rhythm of the angels' beat.

The angels are trying desperately to get your attention. This message has come to you because angels are trying to communicate with you. Angels communicate with you on a daily basis and all they ask in return is that you listen, feel and see. All they ask from you is that you show them a sign that that you acknowledge them and listen to their angelic guidance.

Signs from your angels could be feathers, songs on the radio, rainbows, cloud shapes, coins, number sequences you see repeatedly on clocks and number plates, any of the guided ideas and inspirations you get in your mind, or simply that someone may say something you need to hear. You need to tune in to the signs and feel what resonates for you.

Every minute of every day angels surround you. Ask them for their help and ask them to show you clear signs that you will understand. You can give the angels your cares and your worries, release your burdens to them and let the angels take them and carry them away for you. You no longer have a cross to bear all on your own; angels are here. They are around you, supporting you and guiding you. They protect you and love you.

Angels love you unconditionally no matter what you have, haven't or think you have done. Angels will never abandon you; all you need to do is ask and give them permission to do their work and help you today.

Engage, interact, play with and listen to your angels' signs today. Angels are there guiding you always. They are not restricted by time, space or direction; they can be with many people at once.

Get to know your angels and your guardian angels. Say hi, don't be shy. They are waving back at you and they love you so very much. Give them permission to work with you in your life today.

Angelic Communication Power Words

Put your hands on your heart and say

I communicate with my angels, guides and spirit easily. I hear, feel or see their messages clearly.

Be Willing to Change

Are you resisting change? Are you resisting moving forward?

Change ushers in new energy, new ideas and new inspirations, and opens wonderful new doors for you to walk through if you so choose.

Dear one, are you resisting change? Are you afraid of change? Are you afraid to let go, release and heal? Fear not, dear one, for change is inevitable and part of the natural process of life.

Dear one, you are being asked to be willing and open to change. Just be willing to let change in. Slow and gentle change is required of you, dear one. You are being asked, are you ready to walk the path of change, the path of truth, and be willing to change?

Change is calling, dear one. From deep within your soul comes a longing, a calling that you need to change, to stand up and to just be willing to let change come calling at your door. When it does, will you be ready to open that door? As Mahatma Gandhi said, 'Be the change you wish to see in the world.'

Dear one, change has come knocking at your door and you now must be willing to open that door and let the winds of change blow through you like a breeze on a mild autumn day. This change is your calling – a calling to heal, release and let go.

Change is here to take you on a deep journey of self-discovery and self-love. Change is here to open your eyes and create awareness in your life, which will lead you on a journey to the depths of your soul where you have resisted to go until now because of fear and because you are not sure what you might find there. The angels assure you, dear one, the only thing you will find there at the very core of your soul is love, but you have to be willing to let go, become unstuck and let change blow over you.

Change is scary – it brings fear of the unknown – but change is also empowering and liberating. It sets you free to be the person you are meant to be. Change will challenge you, it will force to you be flexible, witty, open and flowing, moving like the trees in a in a breeze, whose branches need to be pliable, flexible and able to move every which way or they will snap, break off and die.

Fear not change. Fear not the new. Fear not the path you are about to walk. Instead fear being stuck, stagnant and unable to move forward, for this is what will keep you in vibrational prison.

Change is knocking at your door, angel. Open the door and let change in. Be willing to implement change in your life today. Take responsibility for your life and where you are going; don't just let the wave dump you on any shore but jump inside your internal navigation system and steer change into your being today.

Change is here: embrace it, work with it and be it. It's time to move it and shake it. Let go of resistance and make little steps towards change today. Keep moving forward, keep an open mind and heart, and go with the flow, but always be the one charting the direction of your ship.

Change will bring in the positive new energy required to challenge you to let go of beliefs and emotions that no longer serve you and that keep you stuck in vibrational prison. It's time to change and raise your vibration today.

Be Willing to Change Power Words

Put your hands on your heart and say

I am open to the possibility of change and welcome change into my life now.

Healing

You are on or about to embark on the healing journey of a lifetime to shift, heal, transmute and awaken your soul. You are a powerful healer. You are healing.

Healing is about going deep within your very core and dealing with it all, though not all at once. Sift through the layers, like when you peel the skin off an onion one layer at a time. How deep are you willing to go? Dear one, this is a very personal message as it has to do with self-healing. It wants to give you a gentle nudge or a push to journey deep within your heart to awaken the power that lies within, and to take you on your healing journey. A healing guide awaits.

Healing guides are patient. They wait for you to help you go deep within yourself to see what it is you need to heal, release, let go of and shake off. Your healing guide wants to help you change your old, out-dated beliefs and empower you to be who you are meant to be.

Your healing guides know everything about you – your hopes, dreams, fears and doubts – and your healing guides know your pain and grief, for they help to carry it for you when it gets too much.

It is now time. Your healing guide wants to take you on amazing journey of self-discovery right down to your very core, to take you back to childhood and past events to help you heal, grow and forgive yourself and others. This message is deep, dear one, really deep. The angels and your healing guide want you to heal your life and free yourself from hurts, regret, unforgivingess, limitations, old beliefs and fears. It is time for transmutation and letting go of what no longer serves you and is only playing out in your life negatively. It is time to usher in the new, dig deep and renew. You are a powerful healer, dear one, but in order for your gift to shine through crystal clear you must be willing to walk your talk and not just give good advice, because your advice is actually often meant for yourself.

If this message feels harsh for you right now, it's because it is pushing buttons that you knew were there but didn't want pushed. It's ok, dear one. This message is a timely yet gentle reminder that it is time for you to push down further on your healing journey and go where you haven't gone before. Sift through the layers one by one, be proactive and listen, and your healing guide will help you and guide you to people, places, books and supports than can help you.

This message is asking you to prepare for your journey, for your time has now come to connect with your healing guide and go down further than you have gone before. Don't be afraid, dear one. You are fully supported. Go gently, love and nurture yourself always, and open up to the arms of healing from within.

Healing Power Words

Put your hands on your heart and say

I am open to healing. As I heal every part of me, my heart opens and I am free.

Crystals

Crystals are living, breathing powerhouses with a magnificent vibration. They have come here to serve, help, support, nurture and download information to you. Crystals are so, so healing and gentle to work with.

Did you know that all the crystals you own have worked with you in a past life and they have come forth to you now so you may work with them again?

Do you have an affinity with crystals, or are you just starting to hear the crystal beings calling your name?

Crystal are so powerful. They love you and being around you. They hold aeons of information and this message has come to you today to help gently make you aware that crystals want to come into your space and work with you if they haven't already. If they are already in your life, then it's time to work with them on the next level.

Ask yourself, what does this message mean to you today? What are the crystal beings trying to communicate to you?

We are the wise ones, the healers, the vibration of love. We are your friends. We are here to support you, help you, heal you and bring you most needed information for you to work with. We want to work with you.

Hear our calling, our soul speaking to your soul. This is our soul speak. Let us in to touch your heart and soul. Do you hear the calling? We are calling you forth now. We are the masters of the earth and you are the creator of the earth. We wish to work with you today.

This message has come to you today because crystal warriors and beings wish to contact you. They want you to work your magic and they can help facilitate this.

Once you work with and experience the powerful, loving vibration of crystals, your life will be changed and radiate in positive new ways.

The crystal beings are calling you today.

Crystals Power Words

Say this with your hands on your heart

I am open to nature's gifts. I use the elements to assist me on my healing journey.

Gratitude

Set yourself a challenge to have an attitude of gratitude every day for the rest of your life.

Pick ten things a day you are grateful for and say them aloud or in your head, or write them down. Create your attitude of gratitude today and magic will happen in your life.

Being in a state of gratitude is magic. You are creating magic, love and happiness tenfold. Imagine every day stating at least ten things you are grateful for in your day; this process fills your heart with love, you become more grateful for all you have and you become focused and present in your reality.

Every day have an attitude of gratitude. Be grateful for the small things, the things you love and the things that make your life easier. Be grateful for life.

Adopt an attitude of gratitude today and love the life you have.

Here are some things you can be grateful for in your life today:

A smile
Your children or grandchildren
Your comfy bed
Your car
Seeing a butterfly
A beautiful flower
Great customer service

The list of things you can be grateful for is endless. Become more positive, immerse yourself in the attitude of gratitude today and pass it on to the world. It's catching and promotes love; it's a beautiful space to be and live in.

Gratitude Power Words

Say with your hands on your heart

I give gratitude and thanks for all I have, all that will be and all that is. I am eternally blessed. My heart swells with gratitude.

Passion

Let passion become you!

Are you, dear one, living your most passionate life? Are you living in your passion every day? Do you know what you are most passionate about? It's time to find your passion and live it every day!

What fills your heart with joy? What makes you sing? What are you passionate about?

It's time to centre yourself, dear one, in your heart space and think of your passion, your heart's truest desire, and get about bringing it out into the world.

What is a life without passion? A sad one! If you have a passion you can nurture it; you have permission. It's about finding balance and working to make it how you want it to be. This is your life; make it a passionate one.

If you are working full time and want eventually to make your passion a full time job, you can! Just take guided action, trust your gut and bring your passion out into the world one step at a time.

We need more passion in the world, for passion infuses love, happiness, energy, and magnificence into your vibration. It is infectious and when it spreads to others it helps them to release their passion.

Angel, sit with your hand on your heart and think of your passion – see it, breathe it, visualise it in your mind's eye and feel it in your heart. What is it and how does it feel?

Now see yourself living and breathing this passion while making an awesome income that fully supports all your needs and pays the bills with enough left over for savings, luxury items and holidays. Visualise all this paid for by your passion. What does it look like and how does it feel?

You just visualised this, so you can create it. It is there; the law of polarity has entered your life. Now dance with this, stay centred in joy and work through your challenges with an open heart and mind, knowing that you are creating the passionate life you deserve and desire. Go forth, dear one, go forth into your passions now!

Passion Power Words

Say with your hand on your heart

I engage in activities that fill my soul with passion. I am passionate about life and all things in my life. Passion drives me forward.

Open

Be willing to be open, dear one. Open yourself up to new possibilities, theories, changes and a new way of living – a new existence – for you are powerful, dear one, and need to be open.

You, dear one, are the wave of the new, bringing forth a powerful new consciousness and new thoughts into the world. You are a light worker. God needs you to go forth now and accept his mission.

Constantly raise, shift, heal your vibration, expand your mind and accept your gift, for new and exciting possibilities are all around you, dancing to the tune of your beat.

Every day there are new exciting things to be done, created, invented and lived. We now ask you to open yourself up to all the wonder, joy, excitement and love that these possibilities bring. These possibilities transform your very being. They encourage, guide, love and support you. Open your arms and receive them now.

Being open is simply being willing to be flexible and let the light shine in and guide your intuition to new and exciting things.

Be open and trust your intuition, for the angels work through you, guiding you to new exciting possibilities. This is limitless living with limitless possibilities.

Be open, receive and stay centred in love, joy and happiness, for these feelings open the gateways for abundance.

Open Power Words

Say with your hands on your heart

I am willing to be open. I am open to receiving all the gifts of the universe. I am open and receptive now.

Forgiveness

Forgiveness of self, forgiveness of others, letting go and moving forward, setting yourself free

It is time, dear one, to forgive and let go. Forgiveness doesn't mean you are saying that what was done to you is ok or all right, but you are saying 'I am no longer going to stay in resistance, stuck, stagnant, bitter, resentful or angry anymore. I simply set you free.'

Ask yourself, dear one, are you stuck in the vibrational prison of unforgivingness, constantly reliving what happened or what was done to you? Are you, dear one, allowing this to affect your life now? Are you letting it stop you from enjoying your life to the fullest moment? Is it robbing you of this present moment because you are stuck in the past unable to move forward?

Dear one, you are loved and you are safe. The angels wrap their wings around you now. Surrender to the love and warmth of the angels, dear one; let it all go. Let all the unforgivingness melt away. Let it go for it's eating away at you; it's toxic. You must now be prepared to move beyond this, and that means taking healing steps to help yourself.

Ask yourself, why am I holding onto this so tightly? Why can't I let it go? Is this serving a purpose for me now in present time and if so, what purpose and why?

Forgive yourself, dear one. You are safe and loved, and you are in a safe place; it is time to open your heart to the powers of joy, love and compassion, and set yourself free to live fully in this present moment. Then new opportunities will open up and you will begin to heal.

Forgiveness is important. Are you ready to open your heart to the healing power of love and set yourself free from the chains that bind you?

Forgiveness is now called forth into your consciousness. Do you choose it? Will you use it to propel you forward into the love and light, and use its power to fulfil your destiny?

The greatest power is moving forward, being happy and setting yourself free, for you are free to do and choose as you please. You are free, dear one, and the choice is yours. Forgiveness is called forth today.

Forgiveness Power Words

With your hands on your heart say

*I open my heart to the possibility of forgiveness.
When I am ready, I set myself and everyone I
need to forgive free. I am in the process
of forgiveness now.*

Abundance

Abundance is simply a state of mind!

Dear one, abundance is yours today if you choose to accept it. What you must understand is that abundance is not just limited to money; it is love, health, gratitude, opportunities, friends and so much more. Ask yourself, what does abundance mean to you?

Abundance will not always show up in the form of money. Sometimes it will be opportunities or things you acquire like a gift, help, friends or energy. What you must realise about money is that money itself is simply an exchange of energy.

Dear one, are you having abundance issues? Become aware, dear one, of the thoughts you think and the words you speak. How do you speak about things in your life? How do you speak about money? If you are speaking negatively, it is time for an energy sweep. To do this you can just say 'cancel, clear, delete' as soon as any negative thought comes to you, then replace it with a positive word, action or thought.

Abundance energy is asking you to become aware of your situation and your state of mind, and realise how abundant you really are, how beautiful your life really is and how many things you have to be grateful for.

You are loved, dear one, and you have unlimited resources from the universe. A simple understanding and shift in consciousness is required here. You may have already begun that shift and now it's just expanding. Every day be grateful for the little things you have, bless your food and give thanks.

Abundance is a state of happiness that is not judged by the material things we own or if we can keep up with the Joneses. Today abundance energy is challenging you to rethink what abundance means to you and how you can shift your perspective to an abundance consciousness.

Dear one, you are already so abundant. Gently open your eyes and look around you, for you will see abundance energy all around you. It's in the hugs from our children, in people's smiles, in people's actions and in our food. We have plenty and there is enough for everyone. You are provided for from an unlimited source: the universe, God and the angels.

Open your arms and accept abundance energy into your life from this day forward. You are an abundant creator of the universe. The words that you speak and the thoughts you think are creating a living vibration, a beacon resonating out into the universe and magnifying this back to you. Anchor your energy into an abundance consciousness and start living abundantly today, for you are and always have been abundant.

Abundance Power Words

With your hands on your heart say

I have enough and I am enough. Unexpected money simply shows up and I am grateful for all the blessings and abundance I receive in my life daily.

You Are Worthy and Deserving

You are worthy and deserving of all your heart's desires!

Angel, sometime in your life – or maybe many times – someone told you that you are not worthy and deserving, and you believed them! Angel, this is not true. We angels are here to remind you that you are worthy and deserving. You deserve happiness, abundance, love and joy. You are perfect, angel, just as you are. Start to love and accept yourself today and know you are worthy and deserving.

Think back, angel; who told you that you were not worthy and deserving? Notice who first pops into your mind when you ask yourself this question; there could be just one person or there could be many. These people didn't really mean this. They were simply projecting their own fear onto you – someone once told them they were not worthy and deserving too!

It's ok to let it go. Cut your cords, release this belief and send it to the light for transmutation because you are so worthy, so deserving and so loved. This belief no longer serves you anymore.

Angel, go forth knowing you deserve every bit of happiness, love, abundance and opportunity coming your way. You are a good person. You are an angel. We love you.

You are loved and you are worthy and deserving. Know this; let it sink into the core of your very being. Know that today and from this day forward you will now believe this and remind yourself that you are worthy and deserving. Let this negative belief go, reprogram your consciousness to believe you are worthy and deserving, and know this for the rest of your days. Live with purpose, let people know you are here and be empowered!

You Are Worthy and Deserving Power Words

With your hands on your heart say

I am worthy and deserving of love, happiness, abundance and life. I am enough for all situations in my life. I love me for who I am.

Love

Love without judgments. See through eyes of love. Come from the loving space of your heart.

Love, love, love, love, love is the answer that everybody seeks. All people, including you, angel, want to be loved.

Love is a powerful form of expression. We all want it, we all seek it and we all need it, for we could not survive without it. Without love, our very existence would cease to be. Self-love is so important, dear one. Can you look into your own eyes in the mirror and say
'I love you, _____. I really love you'?

Angel, you need to love and accept yourself. Practise loving and accepting yourself daily, for you first need to love yourself before you can love another. When you can say to yourself 'I really love me, support me and honour me' and hold yourself in high regard, you know you love yourself.

You have permission to love yourself. In fact it is encouraged, for in order to survive self-love is so important. Practise daily looking into your eyes in the mirror and saying '_____, I love you, I really love you and I am proud of you.' Practise this daily and magic will unfold; you will transform your life. This is not vain; this is where you should start with self-love. You have permission to do this from us, your angels.

Love is the answer the world seeks; love is the answer you seek. Practise love on a daily basis: speak love in your words, show love in your actions, start to open and expand your heart, love yourself and express the language of love. Compassion, forgiveness, patience, tolerance and acceptance are all languages of love. Love yourself and love will be magnified back to you tenfold. Extend your love to all earth's inhabitants. Love is practised through kindness, without judgments, without conditions and without limitations. Love yourself like this, angel. Live your life based from your heart space. Thoughts and feelings are just an illusion; you don't have to react to them. They are just ego trying to break through. Love with strength and conviction, and live a heartfelt, love-based life where all your actions, beliefs and motives are based on love. Make love your biggest motivator today.

Love all, love many, love yourself.

Love Power Words

Put your hands on your heart and say

I am love; I deserve love. I open my heart and receive love in. Everywhere I go today I experience love.

Sensitivity

You are a sensitive being. Honour your sensitivity, accept your sensitivity and nurture your sensitivity today.

Dear one, you are a sensitive being. You are sensitive to foods, beverages, situations, smells and surroundings. It's time to tune in to and become aware of what you are sensitive to today.

Being sensitive is a gift that means you are highly tuned in to source. Keeping your body running clean is essential to this connection to your angels, guides and spirits.

Being sensitive can sometimes feel like a lonely path to walk, or even a boring one. Every time you raise your vibration you become more sensitive and more highly in tune, and the consequences of this become more apparent.

Tune in to this message, dear one. What are you sensitive to? Tune in to all your senses: is it food, noise, pollutants, alcohol, smoking, crowds or energies? All these are signs of being sensitive.

Being sensitive can lead to addictions because we don't know how to cope with being so sensitive. Are you trying to give up something in your life today, be it caffeine, smoking, alcohol or sugar? It's time to seek support based around your sensitivities. Avoid what sets them off and give up addictions slowly; it's time to detox. Seek help from a doctor, naturopath or other health professional if you need to. Do what it takes to fine-tune your body and become a radiant beacon of health, shining brightly with a crystal clear connection to source today.

It's never too late to start, dear one, and you are never too old to start. The angels are here to help, guide and support you for when you wish to start. Exercise, clean eating, drinking plenty of water, changing your thoughts, aromatherapy oils, meditating, breathing, nurturing yourself, self-care, self-love, healing, releasing emotions and rest are all parts of learning about and honouring your sensitivities.

It's ok to be sensitive, for it's who you are. You are now being urged to take great care of yourself, and explore and honour your sensitivity today.

Sensitivity Power Words

Put your hands on your heart and say

*I am a sensitive being. I honour my sensitivities
by listening to my body, mind and spirit.
By honouring me I am being authentic
and honest with myself.*

Harmony

Harmony, dear one, is dancing to the beat of your own drum and living freely by the rhythm of your own beat. This is when you find harmony, dear one, flowing at your feet. Create your own harmony; create your own beat. Be true to yourself, dear one. Dance to your own rhythm – no one else's but yours. Flow with it, go with it, create it and live it.

Harmony will flow endlessly when you create it in your life and dance with all that is in the creation of your life. Each new beat brings a new creation. Find your rhythm, find your beat and you shall find harmony flowing at your feet.

This message comes to remind you that we are powerful creators and we have choice. What we choose will come about and what you seek shall come to pass, so be sure to deliberately create what it is you actually desire.

Harmony Power Words

Put your hands on your heart and say

I choose to live in harmony with myself. I choose peace and I choose love. There is peace within my heart, mind and soul. Peace is a state of mind I choose, peace is a feeling I choose and peace swells and dwells within my body.
I activate peace now.

Sit with this, dear one. What does peace feel like for you?
Notice the feeling and let it fill your whole being until
you feel nothing but peaceful, calm and centred.

Joy

Joy sits within every organ of your body; it runs deep within your soul. What is joy, you may ask; it's the feeling of fullness, contentedness, happiness and passion. It's the spark that drives you and fills your very being with love. It's your driving force, your why!

Angel, we all need to hold the vibration of joy! If you are not joyful, sit quietly with your hand on your heart and ask yourself why. Say to yourself, 'What will bring me joy? What will bring me that spark, that driving force that I seek?' Listen quietly and patiently to your answer and then allow yourself to get a divinely inspired plan to create the joy in your life that you seek.

It's up to you to bring in the vibration of joy, own it and channel through the divine the joy you seek and deserve. It is safe to follow joy and you deserve joy, so go forth now, dear one, and create the joy you seek. Let go of limitations: let go of the whys and limiting beliefs. If not now, angel, when? When will you create the driving force and fill your soul with the vibration of joy? Passions run wild, angel. Passion equals joy. We are to live, laugh, love and be happy. Bring joy into your vibration today! Now go forth into joy!

Joy Power Words

Put your hands on your heart and say

I am joyful and I am grateful for my family, friends and all I have. When I think of these things joy fills my entire being. I am safe, loved and supported.

Compassion

Compassion for one another, compassion for self, compassion for the world, compassion for all living things

Dear one, hold compassion in your heart always. Hold compassion in your hands, hold compassion in your heart and hold compassion in the words you speak, live and breathe. Hold compassion for each other, all living things, the earth, the sun, the moon and the water. Give as much as you can with compassion in your stride, for walking and living with compassion is a gift of the human spirit.

We must hold compassion for one another and show kindness, love and respect on our journeys. Lead the way, for you are a beacon of light radiating compassion. Lead by example and others shall follow. Stand and lead with love, compassion and an open mind and others shall follow you as you walk a path of love and light. Always lead with light so that when you leave, the light will continue to grow and shine out to others on their path.

Compassion Power Words

Put your hands on your heart and say

I hold compassion in my heart for myself, for life and for everyone who needs me to hold the space of compassion. I practise compassion in life for everyone and everything.

Fire

It's time to light your internal flame. It's time to start a spark, for one spark is all it takes to start a fire within your heart. It's time to start your fire and really feel it inside. Your flame, your desire, your burning passion is leaving residue on the inside. It decays with no warmth, sitting dormant and still; it's time to light that fire so you don't remain stagnant and stuck in the sands of time. Your time on earth is precious and you have a gift that needs sharing with the world.

It's time to light that fire and let your light burn bright, for you have nothing to be ashamed about and nothing to fear. You will kick yourself in time to come if you let your fire go out.

It's time to light that fire and shine your flame out onto the world with passion, pride and might. Light your fire so big and strong, let it burn with pride and let the world see your light, for it's time to step out of your darkness and into your beautiful light.

Fire Power Words

Put your hands on your heart and say

I ignite the fire within my solar plexus; I light it up and keep it burning bright. This flame reminds me of my passion, my burning desire to share my gifts with the world. My time is now and as I stoke my fire I remind myself why I am here and what I have to share with the world. My gifts are needed.

Acknowledgements

This book was originally created to be an oracle card deck, which I now believe will be an extension to this book. I created this book to help people unlock their inner wisdom, create peace within their lives and have continued awareness in their own lives. I just love sitting down and connecting with angels to see what messages they will bring forth that are needed at this time. This book is me sitting down, connecting to source, bringing through all that is and trusting in the process. I hope you use this book daily and get what you need from it.

I thank my husband for his continued support to let me pursue my dreams.

I thank my children for being the inspiration to push me to find a better way.

I thank the universe for the continued support it brings into my life.

I thank my mentor, Luanne Simmons, for inspiring me on my journey to grow wings and fly.

I thank my dad for believing me.

I also thank the wonderful Erin, who edited this book with her amazing skills.

Melissa Gibbons
www.angelicearth.com.au